Poems from the 53rd Parallel

an anthology of poems by Staffordshire poets

Edited by
Roger Bloor

Clayhanger Press
Newcastle under Lyme

First Printing, 2021

Published by Clayhanger Press
Newcastle under Lyme
Staffordshire
www.clayhangerpress.co.uk

ISBN-978-1-7398007-0-3

Acknowledgements

'Feed the Birds' and 'Magpie' were first published in *Oblivion* (Clayhanger Press 2021).

'Murmuration' was first published in the *Whittington Parish Magazine* 2014.

'Every scene, even the commonest, is wonderful, if only one can detach oneself, casting off all memory of use and custom and behold it, as it were, for the first time.'

Arnold Bennett

CONTENTS

Poems from the 53rd Parallel

Foreword

The Clayhanger Press 2021 Pamphlet Competition invited Staffordshire poets to submit their poems to be considered for publication as a pamphlet. There could only be one winner and Claire Hughes' submission 'Oblivion' was selected by the judge Diana Cant for publication. There were however many excellent poems submitted by other poets and this anthology is a selection of eighteen of those poems.

The poems I have chosen address a variety of subjects and in a variety of forms, but all reflect the creative talent that is present in this wonderful county of Staffordshire. For those of you unfamiliar with the county, what better description could there be than this extract from Chapter 1 of 'The Old Wives' Tale' by Arnold Bennett.

'... They were, for example, established almost precisely on the fifty-third parallel of latitude. A little way to the north of them, in the creases of a hill famous for its religious orgies, rose the river Trent, the calm and characteristic stream of middle England. Somewhat further northwards, in the near neighbourhood of the highest public-house in the realm, rose two lesser rivers, the Dane and the Dove, which, quarrelling in early infancy, turned their backs on each other, and, the one by favour of the Weaver and the other by favour of the Trent, watered between them the whole width of England, and poured themselves respectively into the Irish Sea and the German Ocean. What a county of modest, unnoticed rivers!

What a natural, simple county, content to fix its boundaries by these tortuous island brooks, with their comfortable names — Trent, Mease, Dove, Tern, Dane, Mees, Stour, Tame, and even hasty Severn! Not that the Severn is suitable to the county! In the county excess is deprecated. The county is happy in not exciting remark. It is content that Shropshire should possess that swollen bump, the Wrekin, and that the exaggerated wildness of the Peak should lie over its border.

It does not desire to be a pancake like Cheshire. It has everything that England has, including thirty miles of Watling Street; and England can show nothing more beautiful and nothing uglier than the works of nature and the works of man to be seen within the limits of the county. It is England in little, lost in the midst of England, unsung by searchers after the extreme; perhaps occasionally somewhat sore at this neglect, but how proud in the instinctive cognizance of its representative features and traits!'

I hope you enjoy this anthology and agree with me that these poems from the 53rd Parallel are neither 'pancake' nor 'exaggerated wildness' but fine examples of the excellent poetry which continues to be produced within the boundaries of this proud county of Staffordshire.

Roger Bloor
November 2021

Sandstone and Clay

Written in celebration of Staffordshire Day 2020

Some say there is no accent in Stafford – so travel ten miles south to submerge y'self in broad Cannock and Black Country accents and dialects.

Take thee-sen seventeen miles north where the Potteries accent rolls softly off tongues, as smooth and streamlined as the edges of a Portmeirion vase –

And you'll be intrigued by the mystery, in these voices, of so much history, to resurrect.

Frequent the follies, landscapes and grounds of Mow Cop, Biddulph Grange or Shugborough estate, explore a ruined castle in the county town or dine at the Swan Inn where Dickens disparagingly once stayed!

Find yourself lost in the wilds: climb gritstone Roaches in the Staffordshire Peaks, ride bikes along reclaimed railway tracks or explore the Staffordshire Moorlands.

On Cannock Chase breathe the scent of dewy pines, hear a woodpecker at work, and watch the sun

Rise over valleys as sleepy animals awake.

Damp cuckoo spit idles around ankles on a brisk morning walk, and clay puddles splash sticky mud on wellington boots.

Sedimentary sandstone at the southern tip of the county glows fiery red, where

Hillforts, rock caves and houses are deeply carved in cliffs at Kinver Edge.

I could talk for hours about our county; explore fields of coal and all the villages and towns...

Recall rural stories from farmers, and miners who worked underground...

Except, the only phrase that remains, is to say that Staffordshire is home.

Mel Wardle Woodend

Once upon a time

Our little, battle-hardened, castled
County town had heart bypass surgery,
her traffic-ravaged centre paved
for gum and stubbed-out butts.
They have left her skirt to spread itself
and sprawl along the river bank.

Middle-aged and slightly dowdy now
she still offers unexpected charms:
some medieval pews, a gilded clock,
the serious Old Court House
with its underground cell and iron bars
and those ominous creaking stairs.
And a leafy graveyard where stones lean
like tired sentries guarding the centuries.

The Ford has gone but the Sow still flows,
now concrete-channeled, washing away
slow days and memories of wild swans
and lazy cows drinking at dusk,
content with waving long ranunculus
and little floods of temper now and then.

Bert Flitcroft

All this I remember

Blue marks on shoulders and on arms
were outward signs the miners had inhaled
the dust which settled in the lung.
Noxious dust, from both the coal and stone
foretold a suffocating death,
          A pitiful pension paid to wives

this I remember

The Blythe Bridge factory men
had ulcers in their nose
from fumes of chromium used
to plate the shiny kettles, pots and pans.
Cancer brought to workers who
          risked all to hold their job

this I remember

Five miles away, a factory set in countryside,
cups, casseroles and china plates,
were decorated with lead paint which,
carried on the brushes and the lips of paintresses
destroyed the red blood cells.
          Pale workers cast aside

this too, I remember

Mike Fisher

The Same View

In winter, a blanket of snow
Can shape and change familiar landmarks
And though it is not winter
And I am not seeing through a veil of snow
The futuristic curved roof of a new leisure centre,
An oblong grey supermarket,
And modern red brick flats opposite my home
Obscure what was once my view of green trees lining the river.

I know they are all still there –
Taller, even more majestic than twenty years ago:
Weeping Willows drape themselves gracefully over the river
Shielding a heron and the pair of swans who have made their nest,
Silver Birch bark shimmers
Casting dappled shade onto the grass bank where picnickers sit.
These trees lined the riverbank where a teenage me played football.
They are still there, and I am still here
Even though my view has been blurred by buildings
        I can see everything
                When I close my eyes.

Mel Wardle Woodend

Motorway Services

We have Harthill, Sandbach and Norton Canes,
Or Keele perhaps, then Hilton Park,
Oases on our arid motorways
Where cars pull in and drivers dash
To pay a welcome visit to the loo.
They might pick up some sort of snack;
A ham baguette at four pounds sixty-five?
Bizarrely, no one seems to mind.

Some seem to have a quite poetic ring;
Maidstone and Medway, Michaelwood,
Yet are prosaic like all the rest,
All brash and bright and overpriced.
Outside the ladies' loo men hang about
For wives who always have to queue,
The atmosphere there nervously frenetic,
A place you wouldn't loiter long.

Pease Pottage, Taunton Dean and Clacket Lane
Are all quite soulless, lacking charm
Despite romantic, classy sounding names,
Which don't excuse their petrol prices.
It hardly matters then which one you pick,
They serve a function and that's it;
Pee, tea, coffee, cake, hit the road again.
Repeat every one hundred miles.

Malcolm McMinn

Summer Offensive on the River Dove

I came upon a late-summer field,
newly mown and set high above a gorge
scored through the limestone plateau.
Cylinders scarred the bare ground:
fresh grass, machine-rolled, taut
with menace and sullen with intent,
arrayed like army tents or as if Paul Nash
had assembled here an armoured regiment.
They crouched mechanised and ready to roll:
a surprise attack upon the trippers
splashing in the river far below.

Splayed under a harsh surrealist sun
the shorn field was stretched botox tight,
ricked in anticipation for the fight to come.
Stubbled ridges marked the axis of advance;
the sheep were long gone to slaughter.
Above, on telegraph wires, the swallows danced
a nervy look out, anxious for the starting gun.

I was in a walking gang; they sensed something
wrong and threw a sideways glance.
'That's weird,' said one. 'It's strange
the way that field is so uniformly arranged.'
But only I, the birds and the armoured grass,
could know the plan of attack,
knew all was well on track,
for this, the coming summer campaign.

Mark Johnson

Murmuration

Overhead
light absorbing clouds
spit spite and
stinging rain.
They can't hide the churning dance,
feathers rush to bed.

Leaden skies
bringing early night,
oppressive,
depressive,
surely prompts the tumbling romp,
wings prepare to sleep.

From Autumn
to following Spring
the least loved garden bird
creates the best loved display,
starlings murmurate.

Jo Woodward

Latent

The kestrel hung like a knife, sharp
over a membrane of late-afternoon light
stretched taut and shimmer-bright across
Goldsytch Moss.
                              To either side
the last great slip and dip of the Goyt syncline
twisted,
      dissolved,
            resolved itself then climbed
one final time into tangled towers of quartz.

Three years since I had come into this land;
yet I felt that moment as if time had stopped
and I was suspended between two worlds:
one this ragged Moss; the other not.

The kestrel hung one moment more.
Then dropped.

Mark Johnson

Watching Buzzards on a Spring Day

Spring calls you again,
the common who once wasn't.
The warm air rising
lifts you higher becoming
pinioned flecks before the clouds

wings stretched, inviting,
gathering your partner.
The wind as music,
you whirl, twirl, slide and glide,
dancing across ballroom skies.

Jo Woodward

Our walk by trees

Close to the old gates, we left the car.
Along the path, across the river, grubby and slow,
Passed the church and through the kissing gate.

Near to the wood, we climbed the style,
The trees had shed their leaves, now trampled underfoot.
Ahead the fence was breached, the wire mesh bent right back,
On hands and knees, we scrambled through, first you then me
Surprised! we laughed and squeezed each other's hand.

Along the path, we hoped to see the deer - none came.
Steep between the trees we reached the ridge
Less short of breath than we expected for our years.
Seven ancient beech, the trunks misshapen, gnarled,
Alive before our birth, they'll oversee our passing.

We wandered on, mature trees left behind,
Searched out the newly planted saplings
Labelled 'Charlie' 'Will' and 'Christopher'.
Sound roots now set to grow, branch out and soar
Growth we will see for all too short a time.

Few other walkers to intrude, disturb a closeness,
Memories, joys and sorrows shared
Retrace our steps, back to the waiting car.

Mike Fisher

Reverse Alchemy

'I am fond of you,' she said.
Then the inevitable, inexorable 'but'
'but only as a friend.'
'Friend' fell like the auctioneer's gavel
that proves the attic heirloom
so much brummagem brass.
Batter my heart two-timing woman.
I'd rather be hand bagged, yelled at,
kneed in the groin,
than belittled to well-wishing, hand-shaking
scribbler of paltry Christmas cards.
I don't do second place.
It's gold or nothing for me.

As she turned and clickety-clicked away
I made a promise, a solemn promise,
to take it as her test of my resolve.
You see, it isn't in her gift.
Reverse alchemy? There's no such thing.
A thousand and one spells complete
with phials, alembics, choired incantations
can't convert a lover to a friend.

Oliver Leech

The Garden

We sat in the garden
The day after we heard the news
And talked.

The sun shone
Illuminating the beauty of flowers
He had cultivated.

An unassuming man.
Quietly spoken.
So we were quiet too
In our reminiscing and laughter.

The funeral was not where
We said goodbye.
It was there, in the garden,
That we started to let go.
Drawing strength from each other.
Surrounded by love.

Wanda Pierpoint

Magpie

I am the magpie of broken things,
I will not be contented with golden rings or silver spoons,
I refuse to be blinded by the sunlit shine of diamonds and
I will never adore pearls that burn with silver,
So I throw them out.
Watch them fall and crack like eggs.

Into twigs and leaves I weave the dying
Dandelion that lived in the egg cup;
Add our stone collection, cardboard castles,
Sea shore shells, fridge magnets and the novelty
Socks you got me for every single birthday.
I wrap each strand around the cracked spine
Of *Peter Pan.*

Yes, I rescued him. Lifted him from the rubbish heap
Where he lay after failing to lull you to sleep,
When you abandoned the quest to remain a boy
Forever.

I stitch every dull treasure with the loose thread of
Memory and tie them together with one of my own
Clipped feathers. Weighed down by fingerprints,
My construction leaves me with nothing more than an
Empty nest.

Claire Hughes

Air Raid

It's dark in here
Cold and damp
No light allowed
Safe

I still hear drones
Visualise exploding lights
Taste acrid dust
Smell charred flesh

It's dark in here
The lights have gone
Stay still
Invisible

Some dark never leaves
Insidious
Invades the mind
There is no respite

Strike a match
Ignite my dress
Whirling flames
Dancing, enticing

Bathed in glorious hues
My light
Expires

Wanda Pierpoint

Picking Fruit

'When picking fruit, don't take them every one.
Be generous and let some hang upon
the branch for those who later walk this way
and some to feed the birds another day.'

Basket brim full, limbs aching, skies looming.
'Time to go,' I heard, 'time to go.'
But then I saw it,
a fruit so juicy plump, so fleshy rich.
In low light beams it glistened, taunting.
I was transfixed, transformed,
a burglar who spots much better loot next door,
a chancer slipped some insider tip.
I stretched but could not reach,
paused, drew breath, stretched again.
If those thorns were poison tipped,
if there were adders in the grass ...
I measured, moved. I tiptoed on a tussock,
reached, leapt,
fingertips touching, feathering.

Boots muddied, pricked and nettled
I clambered out of the ditch.
Now I knew
why Napoleon marched on Moscow,
why Icarus flew so high
 'Time to go!' they shouted.
I'd be back next day.

Oliver Leech

Feed the Birds

The blackbird arrives at the window, a dust of spring dew on
his inkblot feathers. He opens his fire breath beak, says please
and thank you, but I have nothing. No scraps or seeds, no
flesh left over from their morning fruit. My cough sends him
through the apple blossom where he rests on the empty bird
feeder. Dust settles on the bare shelves, I think I have been
granted silence but, when I turn, I am greeted with the beaks
of two more.

a bounty of food;
treasure we all should find and
be willing to share

Claire Hughes

Ode to Arnold Bennett

He was that rarest of things,
a man who fully mastered his art,
who could weave the intricate warp
and the weft of the human heart,
the best and the worst of it.
An artist who painted the human soul:
the hidden currents and depth
and submerged rocks of it,
the sunlit glades and uplands
and the shades of happiness.
Here was a man who understood
how we suffer the paradox of love;
the sweetness and the gall,
the endless give and relentless take,
the pull and power of it
and the spell it holds over us.
The strength of family ties and the lies
we utter in its name, the soft pain,
the grand gesture and the grind,
the prize and the high price of it.
Here was a compassionate sage,
a man who understood we love love itself.
Who loved words as if mining for gold,
who embraced the new, the need for the old.

Bert Flitcroft

I Wish

I wish my poetry was free
Of all restraint and ancient rules,
Rejoicing in its liberty,
Abandoning tradition's fools.

Of all restraints and ancient rules
Our modern poet's not encumbered,
Abandoning tradition's fools
He states the sonnet's days are numbered.

Our modern poet's not encumbered;
His verses soar like any bird.
He states the sonnet's days are numbered
While villanelles must not be heard

His verses soar like any bird,
Devoid of form and sometimes metre
While villanelles must not be heard
Or quatrains, which, some think, are neater.

Devoid of form and sometimes metre,
Rejoicing in its liberty
Of quatrains, which some think are neater,
I wish my poetry was free.

Malcolm McMinn

The Poets

Bert Flitcroft lives in Lichfield. He has three collections of poetry published, most recently *JUST ASKING*. He is a prize-winning poet, has been Poet in Residence at the Southwell Poetry Festival and has performed at a number of national festivals including amongst others The Edinburgh International Book Festival, Stoke and Birmingham.
He has been Staffordshire Poet Laureate and worked as resident poet with one of our 'National Treasures', The Wedgwood Collection at the V&A, with the prestigious RIBA exhibition 'The Road Less Travelled', and recently as part of the University of Keele project 'Labelling the Museum'.

Mike Fisher was born in Birmingham and blessed with teachers who introduced him to Shakespeare and poetry alongside science A levels. Following Medical School in 1968 he moved to Stoke on Trent, dividing his time between General Practice and Postgraduate Teaching. He was awarded an Honorary Doctorate by Keele University in 2017. Writing poems is a joy made richer by sharing them with the Newcastle Stanza Group, with whom he has published some.

Claire Hughes is a Birmingham born writer now living in Staffordshire. She completed her MA in Creative Writing at Lancaster University and her poetry has been published in magazines such as *One Hand Clapping*, *192* and *The Babel Tower Notice Board*. She has also had her poems featured in anthologies by Dream Well Publishing and the Mum Poem Press anthology, *Songs of Love and Strength*. Claire is now working on an experimental novel. Her first pamphlet *Oblivion* is published by Clayhanger Press.

Mark Johnson is a writer based in Leek in the Staffordshire Moorlands. He is fascinated by the relationship between landscape and mind, (not always his own).

Oliver Leech is a retired teacher, native of and life-long resident in North Staffordshire. He now tries his hand in poetry, philosophy, calligraphy and art, and his book *Quandaries,* a collection of poems, calligraphy and artwork, was published in 2020 by Clayhanger Press. He has had poems included in the *Newcastle Stanza Group Anthology 2020*, also published by Clayhanger Press.

Malcolm J. McMinn is retired, having spent his working life in the ceramics industry. He took up writing poetry as a retirement hobby, and his other interests in life include classical music, walking and photography. He particularly enjoys his membership of the Stoke Stanza. Malcolm is quite eclectic in his subject matter and tends to use traditional forms such as sonnets, sestinas, villanelles etc. As his pantoum 'I Wish' indicates, he finds writing free verse difficult, but keeps trying.

Wanda Pierpoint was born in Birmingham and from an early age she would make up and tell stories to her siblings and cousins. Her first job was at Cadbury Brothers where she learnt how to type and do shorthand – skills which have been invaluable. She married, moved to Tamworth, had two children and then qualified as a teacher. She continued to tell stories to her pupils and one, about a dragon, was published in 2019. She has written several children's stories and is currently working on a novel. Reading and writing have always been an integral part of her life.

Mel Wardle Woodend is Staffordshire Poet Laureate 2019-2022. Her published work includes several dyslexia-friendly children's poetry and story books, a poetry collection *Natural Colours* (2017) that explores the concept of synaesthesia, and *Just a Thought* (2019) exploring themes of mental health. Mel holds an MA in Creative Writing with Merit, is one half of WORD Stafford and enjoys facilitating poetry workshops, participating in slams, open mics, and festivals.

Jo Woodward lives tucked away in a little-known corner of Staffordshire somewhere between Lichfield and Burton. She spends her days hating to do housework, talking to her cat or her husband, staring out of the window or in the garden contemplating the fluff in her navel.

Index of Poets

Index of first lines

Cover Design by Clayhanger Press

Typesetting and Design Roger Bloor
Senior Copy Editor Sara Levy
Assistant Proofreader Adam Lampert

www.clayhangerpress.co.uk

Printed in Great Britain
by Amazon